THOMAS KINKADE

Twenty-Five Years of Light

SUNSET ON LAMPLIGHT LANE

THOMAS KINKADE

Twenty-Five Years of Light

**Andrews McMeel
Publishing, LLC**

Kansas City

Cover image: *Stillwater Bridge*
Back cover: *Elegant Evening at Biltmore*
(Permission to use this image is graciously provided by The Biltmore Company.)
Sleeping Beauty Castle and Cinderella Castle and other Disney properties © Disney

08 09 10 11 12 LIB 10 9 8 7 6 5 4 3 2 1

Library of Congress Cataloging-in-Publication Data

Kinkade, Thomas, 1958-
  Thomas Kinkade : twenty-five years of light / Thomas Kinkade. -- 1st ed.
    p. cm.
  Includes index.
  ISBN-13: 978-0-7407-8013-4
  ISBN-10: 0-7407-8013-1
  1. Kinkade, Thomas, 1958---Catalogs. I. Title.

ND237.K535A4 2008
759.13--dc22

2008019133

www.andrewsmcmeel.com
www.thomaskinkade.com

Thomas Kinkade: Twenty-Five Years of Light was produced by Lionheart Books, Ltd., 5200 Peachtree Road, Suite 2103, Atlanta, Georgia, 30341.

Design: Carley Wilson Brown

"*I Believe*

we all have a greater purpose to our lives than merely existing day to day. Each of us, in our own unique way, is called to let our light shine. The unique, one of a kind canvas of our existence is meant to be an inspiration to others—a true joy to behold and a heaven-sent blessing to those we meet and to the world around us."

Thomas Kinkade

The Guiding Light

"Happy accidents, remarkable coincidences, and even painful experiences over the course of my life have nudged me in the direction I needed to go, day by day, year by year. I have observed with awe as circumstances—combined with my own choices (even my own mistakes)—have brought me to where I am today."

Chapter One

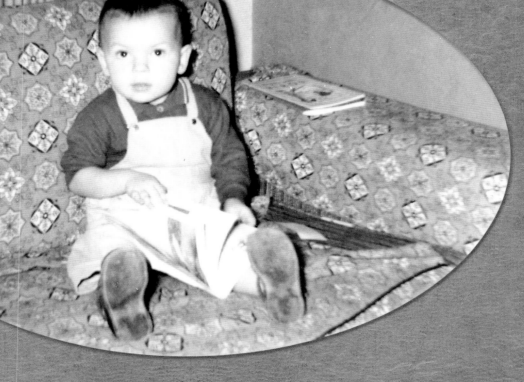

GROWING AN ARTIST
The Early Memories

PLACERVILLE, 1916

THOMAS KINKADE, THE MAN WHO WOULD BECOME

America's most-collected living artist, the man who is known today simply as the Painter of Light,™ was born in Placerville, California on January 19, 1958. Raised in a single-parent home with his mother MaryAnne, sister Kate, and younger brother Pat, Thomas came from humble beginnings. It was during those early formative years when the first seeds were planted that would ultimately shape the way the artist sees the world and effortlessly conveys those feelings onto canvas.

Nicknamed "Old Hangtown" for the number of hangings that took place there in the 1800s, Placerville is filled with an abundance of history, as it was the central hub for the Mother Lode region's mining operations during the Gold Rush. By 1958 the quaint community, which is located in the western foothills of the Sierra Nevada Mountain Range, looked like something straight out of Norman Rockwell's America. Thom's early life in the historical city consisted of a mix of mischievous antics, churchgoing, and a burgeoning love for art that began to take root the moment he first grabbed hold of a crayon. Placerville offered a safe place to grow up and explore. At eight o'clock in the evenings the sidewalks rolled up and it became family time for the community, as people gathered in their homes, lights brightly shining to the outside, to talk and create their own entertainment. It was in this environment that Thom was given the pace of life that allowed him to grow and nurture his talent. "Family was everything for us," says his mother MaryAnne. "We stayed together, played together and went to church together."

Thom dressed for church, 1970.

Pat, Kate, and Thom at right, 1969.

The sanctuary of a loving home with a parent who believes "every child needs the room to make mistakes" is one of the greatest blessings that MaryAnne Kinkade gave to her children.

Thom was recognized as having a special gift at a young age. In fact, his second-grade teacher told his mother that he would grow up to be a great artist someday. His burning desire for artistic pursuit surprised his family. In fact, his siblings thought it would "pass in time," but his talent continued to grow undaunted, and nothing was going to get in the way of what he loved doing most. The finances in the Kinkade household weren't abundant, but that didn't stop young Thom from figuring out a way to get hold of his coveted art supplies. From his first job as a paperboy, Thom understood that each paper he tossed into a driveway translated into money that he could spend on his passion. He even recycled the cast-offs of others: old poster board, blank papers, whatever materials were still usable. Thom always found a means to pursue his love. And when he began stretching his own canvases onto makeshift frames that he had built from discarded wood, he found an inexpensive avenue for practicing his talent. As he began to capture his experiences in Placerville on the homemade materials, it was clear that the "light" was shining on young Thom. Clearly, he was bestowed with a God-given gift for capturing his surroundings in an unforgettable, timeless way. "Thom was an artist from the start," recalls MaryAnne. "I didn't understand it, but I knew what he was. And he knew what he was, that was important. I would look at his paintings with amazement because the artistic ability and the perspective were always right. He didn't hesitate a moment. He knew what to do; he knew how it should look. He was constantly trying new things and he stuck with it day and night."

His sister, Kate, ever the encourager, played a role in immersing Thom in the artistic culture of theater and museums on their frequent trips to San Francisco. Kate worked in the Placer County library and often brought home reference materials on other artists for her younger brother to study. By the time Thom turned fourteen, he had an insatiable hunger to learn about art. During this period, he pored over countless biographies of artists old and new, becoming inspired rather than daunted by their hard lives. He wished to emulate everything they did, delving into every detail of their lives, their techniques, and

An early painting

The Kinkade family—Kate, Pat, Thom, and MaryAnne.

Young Thom at an art museum

Thom as a paperboy.

Hometown of Placerville, looking toward the Bell Tower.

"The Two Little Scamps," a drawing of Pat and Thom.

Teenager Thom shown with artwork from high school.

PLACERVILLE UNION SCHOOL DISTRICT
PLACERVILLE, CALIFORNIA

CERTIFICATE OF MERIT

Awarded to ___TOM KINKADE___

in recognition of ___HONOR SOCIETY___

on this ___9TH___ day of ___JUNE, 1971___

By ___Clarence L. Wilts___
District Superintendent

By ___Robert C. Yout___
Principal

An Honor Roll certificate awarded to Thom in the 9th grade.

kitty

One of Thom's many cartoon drawings.

"There was just no doubt that Thom perceived himself as an artist from day one . . . throughout his entire adolescence and obviously still today."
—Pat Kinkade

their travels. Clearly, the prospect of living his life as an artist was fueling the burning desires in the young man from the old town that was just a short drive from Sutter's Mill, the landmark site where gold was first discovered in California. However, unlike the forty-niners who panned the local streams and rivers a century earlier, Thom wasn't looking to strike it rich. At this point, he knew only that he had discovered his passion.

Thom was so intent on drawing that he often excluded himself from family happenings retreating in his bedroom—his "studio" as he called it. It was the place where his ideas unfolded on his easel. Even during his youth, although he loved playing outside building forts, speeding on bicycles, and getting into the typical country life trouble, his brother found it challenging to pull Thom away from his art. "No, no, I've got to draw," Thom would say, "I'm an artist." And before long, the Kinkade household became the quintessential home of an artist. Every room became filled with artwork. There were pictures stored under

his mother's bed. The laundry room was filled with old canvases that were sometimes stacked higher than the clothes, which were often covered in specks of paint. The living room also had works in progress leaning

A Christmas card that Thom drew in high school.

against the walls; and the entire house was engulfed in the unmistakable scent of oil paint. But Thom's family understood that an artist needed nurturing and room to grow, so they made room for him. "My very first memories of him were that he was always doing this sort of thing," recounts Pat, his younger brother by a year-and-a-half. "There was just no doubt that Thom perceived himself as an artist from day one—continuing with that vision, without wavering, throughout his entire adolescence and obviously still today." Kate even offered to give up her bedroom so that Thom could have a larger "studio" to create and experiment in. "While other people were out at football games," says MaryAnne, "Thom was at home painting away. That's what he wanted to do; that's what he loved. And I was just thrilled with it. I was surprised and excited by it; I realized it was a talent given by God. And Thom realized that. He worked hard at it and it just grew and grew."

By the time he entered into his junior high and high school years, the future Painter of Light™ was known around campus as "the artist," sketching hot rods, cartoons, and caricatures of teachers to the delight of his peers. Thom always found joy in his art and found even more by sharing that joy with others. During this period he began experimenting with self-portraits—and wound up completing a series of them with a passion and vigor that were magnetic. Thom dressed for school wearing an old army jacket,

"Impish self-portrait," c. 1973— This was painted during my early years of experimenting with oils. Working from early family photos, I explored memories from the past.

paint-spotted blue jeans and army boots. His hair, which was once long and curly, was now cropped short and close to his head. He looked more like a young U.S. Marine on leave than a typical Placerville teenager of the early 1970s. For Thom, his new look was a statement of individuality, which was a bit shocking for the quiet town that had become a frequent stopping place for travelers heading to South Lake Tahoe. Thom felt it was more important to be himself than fall into the social pressures of conformity often found in

"Once he understood what his calling was, he never let it out of his sight."—Kate Kinkade

high school. With art, Thom found his place in life and an outlet to create and think outside the box, a trait that carried over into every aspect of his life. With art came confidence and a sureness of where he was headed.

"He was so focused from day one," remembers his sister Kate. "Once he understood what his calling was, he never let it out of his sight. Since he was eight or nine he wanted to be an artist. In fact, I don't know anyone else who had that great a grasp on what his life's work should be at such an early age. He was adamant about achieving everything that he possibly could." Some say it was divine providence that paved the way for the introduction of a special mentor into Thom's life—a man who helped change and shape the course of Thom's art, bolstered him in his talent, and helped him blossom as an artist. And to think the man lived just one house down from the Kinkades' Avalon Lane home.

A retired Art Professor Emeritus from the University of California at Berkeley, Glen Wessels was a noted painter in his own right—a painter with a small art studio on his property. One day as he walked along a neighboring property, Thom noticed a construction crew working on a barn. A small barn in Placerville normally wouldn't draw much attention from a teenager, but Thom's interest in it spiked the moment he first learned from the construction crew that

Thom with his mentor, Glen Wessels, at Glen's "barn" studio.

The "barn" studio was one house down from Thom's

the barn was to become Glen Wessels's art studio. Here was a young man who lived, ate, breathed and slept art. The same young man who tossed newspapers into driveways to save up enough money for supplies suddenly came to the realization that he was living right near a genuine art studio—not a bedroom but a real studio! Anticipation grew as Thom contemplated the thrill of meeting a real artist. Before long, he got his chance to meet Glen, see his studio and shares stories with him. Soon, an affinity sprang up between them. The retired professor, now nearing eighty years of age, took the young artist under his wing, and Thom made sure to take full advantage of the special opportunity. From their first meeting on, Thom went to the barn as often as he could, becoming both handyman and apprentice for the credentialed artist. He

cleaned the barn, ran errands for Glen, and simply did whatever he could just to hang around and watch the seasoned artist as he worked. Glen too became quite attached to the aspiring young artist and Thom enjoyed the company of the old professor, seeing him as both a mentor and a father figure. It's easy to see why. Glen had more than sixty years of experience as an artist, educator, writer, and world traveler under his belt. For the next three years, he tutored his young apprentice in all that he knew. Under Wessels's mentoring Thom was able to hone his skills, no longer just learning things from books but refining his talent and focus with the help of a pro.

During those early years in Placerville Thom experimented with a wide array of styles, from Picasso-type abstracts to Dali-like symbolism to realism, exploring every kind of medium possible, including watercolor, oil, pen and ink, and chalk. He used any material he could get his hands on, once even sketching pen-and-ink drawings on the back of discarded placards advertising the El Dorado County Fair. Not only did he explore the varying modes of artistic creation, but it soon became evident that Thom had entrepreneurial skills as well, a trait that emerged with the growing need to sell and market his art. The first painting he sold was at Sugar Loaf Camp, an

art summer camp for grammar school kids in the Sierras. At the end of the week-long camp, Thom offered his watercolor for $10 and it sold on the spot as he informed the purchaser, "Someday that'll be worth something!" While in high school he began sketching beautiful pen-and-ink drawings that sold in the many

"The Hat, Self-portrait,"—In childhood it seemed I had an obsession with hats. I loved this one , made by my mother. This self-portrait is executed in a brushy technique that shows an interest in unusual lighting, as seen in the facial features.

tourist shops in Old Sacramento. But it wasn't until he started sketching quaint cottages and country roads that Kinkade first realized that this was the type of art that the visiting tourists were gobbling up. It was then that Thomas first found his niche—creating art that brought joy and inspiration to people. Up to that point, he had done everything from painting signs for a sign company in Placerville to creating sketches for local newspapers. Thom even painted a Yogi Bear sign that was seen by passing motorists on Highway 50 for more than a decade. Simply put, Thom made every effort to finance his love for the creative life by using his God-given talents to sustain him. And in the process, he was beginning to make a name for himself, at least at the local level.

Although he enjoyed those early gigs in Placerville, Thom wanted to expand his horizons but, unfortunately, the small city in the foothills of the Sierras didn't offer the kind of opportunities the determined young artist with an abundance of talent was looking for. With an academic scholarship in hand, Thom soon chose to leave his lifelong comfort zone in order to further his education. Thom took the advice of his old friend Glen Wessels, who recommended that he undertake his studies at the University of California at Berkeley. In 1976, shortly after graduating from high school, he left the historical town in the woods for the complexity of university life. Although his time was stretched between academics and odd jobs, the young artist still made time to paint. Setting up his studio in a small, dank basement in Berkeley, he filled it with paints and canvases and used this season of his life to further explore the limitless possibilities of oils and acrylics. "I would play with color," says Thom. "I would play with compositional ideas and new brush techniques. Art has always been a form of play for me. It is my

"Portrait,"—During my Berkeley era, I was influenced by Kokoschka, Bonnard, Egon Schiele and others as I painted a series of portraits of friends.

greatest joy." During this time he relished in the thought of painting outside and began to do so more frequently. He had fallen in love with the intoxicating feeling of putting images on canvas in the open air while growing up in Placerville, and this love for plein air—or open air—painting became increasingly important to Thom during his stint at Berkeley, and would be carried with him throughout his life.

"Still LIfe," c. 1978—During my Berkeley phase, I frequently painted still life to study paint techniques.

Berkeley was not just a time for study; it was a period when Thom made many lasting friendships. One of those relationships started the day he met his roommate and fellow artist at Berkeley, James Gurney, who later became the renowned creator of *Dinotopia*. "He was very fortunate that his roommate turned out to be James Gurney," says his sister Kate. "And I don't know if that was just a fortuitous accident or if Berkeley tried to match interests with roommates—I have a feeling the latter is true." The two artists were a constant encouragement to each other, sharing notes on sketching and playing elaborate pranks on fellow students. They had a love for travel and both wanted a chance to see the world. At the time, neither had an inkling that the future would see many of their dreams come to fruition.

After studying at Berkeley for two years, Thom felt as though the school's rigorous academics weren't allowing him enough time to focus on his art, so he transferred to the Art Center College of Design in Pasadena, California, where the majority of the classes were all art all the time—the perfect curriculum to pacify the young artist's cravings. Thom's excitement and enthusiasm about the new school were so contagious that he soon convinced his best friend James Gurney to join him there. They became neighbors at the Golden Palms, an apartment complex in East Los Angeles that housed much of the artist community from the Art Center. While there, Thom was often visited by his brother, Pat, who eventually moved to the same area. "I lived relatively close to him in Los Angeles," recounts Pat, "and we started running in the same circles. He was involved in the Golden Palms circle at that time. That was a pretty amazing group to be with when they got together." The experience of living among fellow artists in close quarters was an experience that has never been duplicated in Thom's life. Fellowshipping with other artists, exchanging techniques and ideas helped to quench Kinkade's surging thirst for the creative and pushed him to new levels of expertise.

Although the benefits of attending the Art Center were obvious, pursuing a creative career was difficult from a financial standpoint. For that reason many of the young artists who lived in the complex had to discover interesting ways to generate income, and Kinkade's plight was no different. In between classes Thom delivered pizzas, sketched for newspapers, and held a few other odd jobs to pay his way. Money was tight, but with the help of others he seemed to always find ways to make ends meet. His sister often sent care packages. "People would help him out along the way," remembers Kate. "Thom has such an ingratiating personality, the type of personality that people trust immediately. He was able to get people to assist him in providing shelter, food, or whatever. He led a very interesting life while he was going to the Art Center." Kinkade and Gurney were also able to find work in the movie industry to pay their bills. They were hired by director Ralph Bakshi as artists for his animated film *Fire and Ice*. This experience trained Thom to draw purely from his imagination when there was no model or photograph to work from. It's a method of creating that he often uses today in his personal art studio in the Santa Cruz Mountains. No matter how difficult those early college years sometimes seemed Thom wouldn't have it any other way. "I have always felt that the creative life is the life that has the greatest meaning," says Thom. "For example, a friend of mine, who was a poet when I was in art school, proudly showed me his journals one day. There were five or six shelves filled from left to right with thick journals densely inscribed with poetry. I asked him if he intended to publish these volumes, which must have contained thousands upon thousands of poems. 'No,' he said, 'creating it was enough.' There is something to that. The mere act of creating is self-sustaining. Enhancing the lives of an audience is an extra bonus."

Although still a student of art, he managed to have some of his original works shown at art galleries throughout the Los Angeles area, and the response was positive. He had discovered the Hudson River School of painters while at Berkeley and was greatly influenced by their vision for landscapes. So while in Los Angeles, he began to shift his focus more and more to painting the romantic, epic landscapes that proved to be the genesis of his distinguished career as the Painter of Light.

"The Alley,"– This was my environment during my years at Art Center—my studio was in a building at the left. The alley still exists and I still take friends and family by this location. Although the alleyway is near the revitalized downtown Pasadena, much urban squalor still exists.

At the easel, 1983.

"The Barn"– Thom's studio in Placerville, 1984–1993.

Thom and Jim Gurney working on "Fire and Ice," 1983.

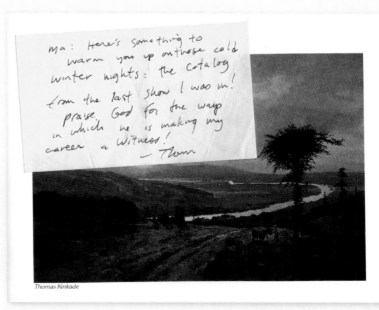

Ma: Here's something to warm you up on those cold winter nights: the catalog from the last show I was in! Praise God for the way in which he is making my career a witness!
— Thom

Thomas Kinkade

Page from the catalog Annual Exhibition and Sale of the Society of American Impressionists, with Thom's note to his mom.

INDIAN CAMP AT SUNSET

Early in my career, I discovered some of my most favorite subjects—the majestic mountains bathed in dramatic light . . . humble homes nestled in a tranquil and natural setting . . . . The Yosemite Valley remains an inspiration to this day.

PASSING STORM, YOSEMITE

PREPARING FOR EVENING

RANGE OF LIGHT

When

I see my life as a series

of unfolding miracles, I'll

always sail forth with hope,

tranquility, and joy

in my heart.

THE OLD WATCHMAKER

NOONING

"The influence a work of art can have is limited by its physical existence. If at some point the painting or its reproductions are gone, its influence is gone as well."

Chapter Two

TURNING ON THE LIGHT

A Published Artist

"I've always felt that most people's lives are filled with enough pain and that very few people have the tolerance to import the pain of others through art. I suppose there is always going to be a market for sad songs, but the greatest hits will always be songs that have you singing in the aisles!"—Thomas Kinkade

THOM'S PHILOSOPHY, THAT ART SHOULD BE A POSITIVE

experience for the audience, something beautiful that lingers on, giving one a moment of respite, was strongly embedded in him by the time he began showing his originals at galleries. He has always desired to have a positive impact on people through what he creates, constantly asking himself, "What is the root motivation to create?" Though both pain and joy are necessary as motivation for the creative act, Thom believed that ultimately it is the expression of joy that is most contagious to the viewer. With this in mind, he began to expand his horizons and broaden the scope of his viewing audience— through works that entice all who study his art.

By now, his work on *Fire and Ice,* coupled with the fact that his paintings at various galleries were growing in popularity, offered him some financial stability and the opportunity to begin seriously thinking about starting a family of his own. In 1982, Thom married his childhood sweetheart, Nanette Willey. At the time Nanette was a registered nurse, and although it was a risky undertaking, the newlyweds decided that it was best for Thom to quit the movie industry in order to devote his attention to painting full-time. His painting in animated films had been a wonderful training ground, but it proved to be very unfulfilling. Thom was frustrated that he was not able to paint the world as he saw it. "Thom began to develop a stronger desire to reflect on the beauty he saw in the world around him," says Nanette. "And the amount of talent he has in his art, he has in so many other areas as well. I knew

Nanette and Thom as newlyweds.

STILLWATER BRIDGE

Thom and Nanette at an early art show.

Thom standing with "Day of Rest," sold at the Biltmore Celebrity Show, for the Biltmore Galleries in Phoenix, 1984.

Invitation from an early gallery showing at Alterman Art Gallery. The featured image, "Birth of a City," is one of three paintings, along with "Dawson," that was produced during Thom's "Blue" period.

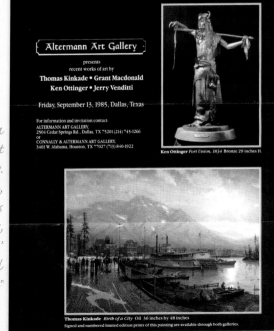

Altermann Art Gallery

presents
recent works of art by

Thomas Kinkade • Grant Macdonald

Ken Ottinger • Jerry Venditti

Friday, September 13, 1985, Dallas, Texas

For information and invitation contact:
ALTERMANN ART GALLERY.
2504 Cedar Springs Rd., Dallas, TX 75201 (214) 745-1266
or
CONNALLY & ALTERMANN ART GALLERY.
3461 W. Alabama, Houston, TX 77027 (713) 840-1922

Ken Ottinger *Fort Union, 1834* Bronze 29 inches H.

Thomas Kinkade *Birth of a City* Oil 36 inches by 48 inches
Signed and numbered limited edition prints of this painting are available through both galleries.

Wallace Road Studio, "The Barn," with early pieces, 1989.

that even if Thom wasn't a painter, he'd be extremely successful." Thom quickly realized that the breakthroughs with his art began to materialize as he started to paint straight from the heart, putting on canvas the natural scenes and images that moved him most.

It was an encouraging and exciting time for the young couple when more of Thom's original oils were being shown at a growing number of galleries throughout California, including the charming seaside community of Carmel, as well as Los Angeles and San Francisco. Although the Kinkades enjoyed the excitement that came from promoting Thom's artwork throughout the Golden State, their hearts still belonged to Placerville. Before long they purchased a property in the historic city that had an old barn on it—a perfect spot for Thom's art studio. Although they had a home and an adjacent place where Thom could go and create, early married life came with plenty of financial worries, even as Thom's work was drawing increased attention. At first, the financial end of his business was slow in taking off. There were many months when no money came in at all. But Thom refused to slow down and continued to forge ahead with his dream. The young artist, who had been quite the entrepreneur at Sugar Loaf Camp selling his first piece of artwork, needed to tap into all of his talents to succeed in the marketplace. "One of the things I admire most about Thom is his ability to not let circumstances dissuade him from his goal," says Nanette. "We stepped

out and took opportunities that logically, if you papered it out, wouldn't work. But there was something in Thom that said, 'This can happen!' It's been such a great experience for me to not only see God's faithfulness but also Thom's ability to stick to his vision."

One area of success in the first two years of Thom and Nanette's marriage came in the form of the paintings that Thom created specifically for galleries. He was fortunate enough to show his work at the prestigious Biltmore Galleries in Phoenix. At that time, he was painting a genre that was more western in style, inspired by his dealer, Steve Rose, who showcased the work of many western-style artists. Thom's luminous landscape scenes, which often included tepees and old western cities, were extremely popular and helped to further establish him as a gallery artist.

But showing originals at galleries where the painting would be bought by a collector

"Dawson of the Yukon"– Thom's first limited edition print, 1984.

and then disappear from public view was not satisfying to Thom. He wanted a much broader audience to be able to enjoy and collect his work. Therefore, the couple decided it was the right time to pursue a long-held dream, that of fine art distribution. In 1984, the couple took their entire life savings of $5,000 and used it to print the first limited edition of one of Thom's favorite Alaskan scenes, *Dawson of the Yukon*. With Thom as the visionary and Nanette as the implementer, they began their small enterprise in their garage and eventually expanded to the point where they could afford a warehouse. Nanette

> "*I would drive up and sit in Thom's barn studio while he painted. He would have ideas and I would have ideas. And out of those casual discussions came the foundation of the company.*"
> —Ken Raasch, Thom's first business partner

ventured out to promote her husband's work. She knocked on gallery doors with prints in hand, and in a short period of time, Nanette helped her husband establish a number of new accounts. "Not having any sales background, it was interesting," remembers Nanette, "because I never felt like it needed any sales. I basically just showed them the art, told them a little bit about our story, and the galleries purchased the pieces. It was really an exciting, new, adventurous time for us. It really took off."

George Carpenter, owner of the Placerville gallery, the first gallery to sell Thom's limited editions, remembers selling Thom's first pieces: "He comes in with a few pieces under his arm—some framed and some without frames—and we set them around the store and lo and behold one sold, then two, and pretty soon three or four sold. And I said, 'Thom, I think we might have something here!' So from that point forward we weren't consigning any

longer, we were actually buying from him." The couple also sold lithographs outside local grocery stores and had huge successes doing it. The sales boom allowed them to print the next piece, and on and on it went as their young enterprise, Thomas Kinkade Fine Art, grew busier. Nanette rolled the prints into tubes and headed to UPS to ship them off. "Every facet of the business was the Lord opening doors," says Nanette. "We were so excited by the success of it, but then shortly became very overwhelmed." Soon, the business grew to the point that the couple needed to hire their first employees. Revenues steadily climbed but it took a chance meeting with Ken Raasch before the business really took off. Ken, who met Thom at the wedding rehearsal of a mutual friend, ultimately proved to be instrumental in creating the fine art publishing and distribution company that would one day help make Thomas Kinkade a household name.

There seemed to be an instant connection of friendship between Ken and Thom. Thom had a clear understanding of his mission to share inspiration with others, and he spoke to Ken about starting an art publishing company. After a few lunch meetings, the ideas were cemented. In 1990, they commenced working on Lightpost Publishing. "I would drive up to Placerville from San Jose where we had started the company in my guest house," remembers Ken. "That was our first corporate office. I would drive up and sit in Thom's barn studio while he painted. We would talk about what we could accomplish and how we wanted the business to be structured. He would have ideas, and I would have ideas. And out of those casual discussions came the foundation of the company. Ideas were formed as to how we were going to position limited editions and the Painter of Light™." They shared the idea that a financially successful business could also be a business that makes a difference in people's lives—business with a purpose far beyond finance. They not only wanted a company environment where the employees thrived and where the highest standards in product quality were held, but they both had a passion to influence culture and society through Thom's art.

Both Thom, the artist, and Ken, the businessman, had a much bigger vision of how art should be marketed and sold than was commonly held in those days. In their opinion, art was not for the elite but for

Nanette in the Kinkade home with tubes of the first limited edition prints ready for shipping, 1984.

Thom and Nanette in front of a grocery store selling prints.

Thom with Linda and Ken Raasch, his first partners in publishing.

Thom on tour with Ken Raasch and Rick Barnett, owner of the first Kinkade stand-alone gallery in Carmel, California.

the common people to enjoy. Art should be easily accessible to all and relevant to people. Thomas Kinkade knew that he wanted to be an artist for the people. With that in mind, the two men decided to bring Thom's art into the collectible arena, a different path from the one that thousands of other art publishers at the time were traveling. Thom and Ken believed that art, ready-framed to be hung up on the wall at the moment of purchase, was a route that would encourage collectible stores to purchase it. And out of collectible stores came the first Thomas Kinkade stand-alone galleries in 1992, a unique enterprise in itself. "In every organization, you've got to have people who play certain roles," says Ken. "And Thom can do it all. He's incredibly unique. Not only can he paint and develop vision and communicate that vision, but he is a very bright businessperson when it comes to the understanding of how to make something successful. It's been a great relationship that has enabled both of us to throw our God-given talents into the pot. I believe that, although marketing is important, most of what we would define as major marketing concepts really were either initiated with Thom or came out of a collaborative effort that the two of us had together. We were quoted in an article I saw as the 'Microsoft of the art business,' and I had to laugh. Every Microsoft has to have a Bill Gates. I wouldn't be the Bill Gates, Thom would be the Bill Gates because that's the creative kind of genius that Thom is."

As Thom's popularity continued on its steady incline, the name of Thomas Kinkade, the Painter of Light™, became more recognizable and his luminous paintings were becoming highly sought after for licensing opportunities. One advantageous alignment was with Bradford Exchange, a collectible gift company and the first to license Thom's work. They had requested Thom to paint an image that could be used for inspiration for the now-famous Hawthorne villages. Thom painted *St. Nicholas Circle* especially for them. It was the homes in *St. Nicholas Circle* that inspired the first structures in Hawthorne's miniature village and it proved to be an amazing success. Sales of the village skyrocketed, catapulting the Painter of Light™ into the exciting world of collectible gifts. By then, it had become clear not only that Thomas Kinkade was marketable but that his paintings were something to behold—special works that drew people in and captivated them.

Bell jar from the Hawthorne Village collection.

Time after time observers of Thom's art comment about their desire to "walk into the painting and live in that house." Reactions like those stem from Thom's innate ability to see with an eye that others do not. When he paints, the skies are a bit more colorful, the greens are a bit more sparkling. Known as a romantic realist, he has the ability to capture the light within the subject. For several years he studied the French impressionists, learning to integrate their sense of movement and brilliance into his own works. In the movie industry Thom learned techniques of painting light while creating animated background scenes. By combining those two abilities with his plein air experiences over the years and the influence that the American luminists had on him, Thom found his style. He was a luminist, the Painter of Light™! This was truly the Eureka moment for the man from California's gold country.

The public was drawn to the simple beauty of his work and amazed at how the scenes seemed vibrant with life when the lights were dimmed or brightened. He had proven himself to be a multidimensional artist: Thom the sketch artist, Thom the plein air impressionist, and Thom the realist. Rick Barnett, owner of the first stand-alone Gallery in Carmel and long-time friend and business associate of Thom, remarks about Thom's abilities: "Here we have an accomplished sketch artist who's very comfortable in that medium, but then can turn around and work in a plein air impressionistic

"This is an artist who is not just an exceptional realist, sketch artist, or impressionist, but is able to work in different color palettes, various subject matters, and from various distances. That's a challenge."—Rick Barnett, Owner of the Kinkade gallery in Carmel, California

Study of Graceland—one of Thom's plein air paintings, 2006.

format. Impressionistic work is remarkable in its complexity, with most of the classic impressionists painting from a set viewing field, but not Thom. He's able to paint from varying distances or viewing fields. And then we take him and put him into a studio and we see that he's able to translate his work into this romantic realism setting, much like a Frederick Church or an Albert Bierstadt with an American luminist style. Not just landscapes, but varying in subject matter—Victorian homes, English cottages, gardens, city scenes, ocean scenes, landscapes. This is an artist who is not just an exceptional realist, sketch artist, or impressionist, but within those umbrellas is able to work in different color palettes, various subject matters, and from various distances. That's a challenge."

It was this vast ability to create art using a wide spectrum of techniques that helped

Thom at work on "A New Day at the Cinderella Castle."

move the American artist to the forefront of such a competitive industry. By the late 1980s, not only were Thom's paintings becoming highly collected—his originals were selling in the six-figure range —but they were also winning prestigious industry awards. In 1989, out of 2,700 entrants nationwide, Thom's

painting *Yosemite Valley* was chosen as the official Collector Print for the National Parks Association, winning the Founder's Favorite award. Eventually that work was reproduced on a rare, 10-dollar collector's stamp.

Thom is often called upon as a favorite commemorative painter of historic places and events. Thom was selected to commemorate the 2002 Olympic Winter Games in Salt Lake City, painting *Olympic Mountain Evening*. He has commemorated Graceland in celebration of its fiftieth anniversary, as well as and the elegant Biltmore Estate. Thom greatly admired Walt Disney, who came from a small town just as Thom had. So when Thom was asked to commemorate the fiftieth anniversary of Disneyland and the thirty-fifth anniversary of Disneyworld Resorts by painting the Sleeping Beauty and Cinderella castles—the two most-recognized icons of our nation's theme parks—it marked a very special, monumental moment in his life. He received the honor of commemorating *Yankee Stadium*™ and *Fenway Park*™, both historic landmarks of America's favorite pastime and beloved by baseball fans everywhere. These paintings were the springboard that ultimately paved way for his entrance into the sports arena, allowing him to paint yet another of his passions: hot rods. The teenager who sketched hot rods for the enjoyment of the other kids became the adult who was granted the honor of painting a commemorative portrait of the fiftieth running of the Daytona 500. Thom has lived out his dreams in ways that few others have.

Thom is anything but one-dimensional. His vision continues to expand into new areas, courtesy of a creative drive that yearns to reach milestones he has yet to attain. His creative talent isn't limited to painting. He has written several books and collaborated with wonderfully talented people on some

of his literary projects. He truly enjoys the collaboration process as it "fires up the juices." Remembering the collaborative work on *Fire and Ice,* Thom says, "We would get together and discuss a scene and talk about how best to stage it, light it, etc. It really is a fun process. Norman Rockwell always said that he would take a good idea from anybody, even the delivery boy bringing by the groceries. You never know where good ideas are going to come from, and I'm certainly not above input." He has also used his painter's eye to create a series of beautiful limited edition fine art sculptures that were well received by the public, thoroughly enjoying the chance to once again play in the clay just as he did back in art school.

For Thom, all creativity is a form of play. French artist Henri Matisse, who was best known for his brilliant use of color, kept the childlike spirit alive throughout his life, and Thom also believes that maintaining a youthful outlook is one of the great gifts of

his life. No matter where he is, he is always creating or dreaming of the next painting, the next project. "I daydream a lot," says Thom. "I'll be sipping my caffé latte down at Starbucks, and an idea will pop into my head. I see things very visually in my imagination and can examine the details one by one in my mind. I make verbal notes to organize what I am envisioning or draw a sketch on any scrap of paper that is handy. That is why I try to continually carry a small sketchbook with me. I'm constantly jotting ideas down. It is fascinating to look back through those books and see page after page of ideas."

The artist who has said that his greatest dream is not to be hung in the Louvre but to be hung in every American living room, the Painter of Light™, whose company now sits on a beautiful campus in Morgan Hill, California, has amply succeeded. Far from being a three-piece corporate product, Thomas Kinkade is a simple man who had a dream and the drive to see it come to fruition. "Thom has always held on to what he thought was right," says Donna Pace, the very first employee of Thom and Nanette's small enterprise in Placerville. "He's had a hands-on approach to his career; and if he felt comfortable going on national TV in a pair of Levi's, then he did, because Thom wanted people to see him for who he is. And even though he has sat with the Pope and had dinner with the President, he's never lost his individuality and his desire to share his joy of art with others."

At Fenway Park during a Red Sox game working on the commemorative painting, 2007.

At the White House with the Clintons, 2000.

On the television set of Good Morning America.

On the movie set of "Christmas Cottage," 2007.

COBBLESTONE EVENING

There are inspiring places I return to time and time again,

and the English Cotswolds are one such favorite destination. I imagine a rambling journey would end here

at that breathless hour when the trout are biting in the brook, and stillness wraps the land in a fleecy blanket of perfect peace.

LAMPLIGHT LANE

SPRING GATE

ELEGANT EVENING AT BILTMORE

My challenge in painting this elegant estate

was not to convey the heroic scale of this fairy-tale castle, but to make it warmly personal.

The Hidden Gazebo

The Autumn Gate

THE VALLEY OF PEACE

Nature has her garden spots; this is one of them.

The golden beauty of aspen trees in the mountains . . . a perfect retreat for the dreamer who lives in all our hearts.

Autumn Lane

ST. NICHOLAS CIRCLE

THE SPIRIT OF CHRISTMAS

Inspired by classic holiday icons

like Currier and Ives, I experience layers of memory as I walk through this Christmas scene.

With

a deep snowpack

on the ground, the warmth

of each of the cabins in this

valley beckons us as the sun

sets low and light plays on

the mountaintops

and melting snow.

WINTER'S LIGHT

OLYMPIC MOUNTAIN EVENING

YOSEMITE VALLEY

DAYS OF PEACE

TETON RENDEZVOUS

Influenced by my work on the theme of the early West

and the American Indians, the mountains and colors seem to tell the whole story of a rugged life in this encampment.

MOUNTAIN MAJESTY

PACIFIC NOCTURNE

Early explorations of mountains and landscapes were the foundation of my continual experimentation with light and color. The light seemed to sparkle on the treetops as I captured this tranquil scene.

LATE LIGHT TAOS

THE BIRTH OF A CITY

Dawson

One of the most detailed paintings of my early career,

this work depicts the famous Yukon town of Dawson during the height of the northern gold rush, around 1898.

FISHERMAN'S WHARF, SAN FRANCISCO

For me, the romance of San Francisco

begins here at this enchanting location . . . so great is the vastness and vitality of this city.

San Francisco, Market Street

A New Day at the Cinderella Castle

A new day

at the Cinderella Castle discovers a

morning every bit as enchanting

as the castle itself.

My celebration

of the fiftieth anniversary of the Magic

Kingdom commemorates the golden

memories of Disneyland so many

children share, as it looks forward to

a new era of imagination

and good times.

DISNEYLAND, 50TH ANNIVERSARY

New York

from a boat on the East River . . .

I was fortunate enough to witness

the seldom-seen views of this great

city. As I savored the panorama of

the Brooklyn Bridge towering above

the glistening city skyline, it dawned

on me: what image could better

summarize the spirit of New York?

In the far distance, Lady Liberty

holds high the torch of freedom

for all to see.

THE SPIRIT OF NEW YORK

EVENING ON THE AVENUE

A nostalgic look back to a time when families strolled America's

Main Streets to mix, mingle, and conduct business, this painting reflects the peace and serenity of the traditional community.

THE HEART OF SAN FRANCISCO

· NEW YORK, FIFTH AVENUE ·

YANKEE STADIUM

GRACELAND, 50TH ANNIVERSARY

"I believe our life is not meant to progress by a cut-and-dried plan, nor by a seat-of-the-pants scramble, but rather an ongoing, interactive process. We sail forward as best we can, we pay attention to the condition of the seas, and along the way, we employ our very best seamanship. But even as we go, we know there will always be a star to steer by, always a lighthouse or buoy to lead us away from total shipwreck, and a storm or two to nudge us onto a different course, or perhaps back onto the course that will lead us home."

Chapter Three

FINDING ADVENTURE

Capturing the Moment

"Everything I experience ends up in the art sooner or later. That is one of the reasons why I have enjoyed traveling. Seeing new places can inspire new visual directions."—Thomas Kinkade

IT STARTED WHEN HE WAS A KID. THOM HIKED AND

sketched in the woods and fields of Placerville. Venturing out into the wilderness and painting went hand in hand for this young artist. Even at an early age, Thom was never comfortable painting from photographs. That was too boring. He wanted his works to come from multidimensional, real-life experiences, not merely from a photo. His mother, MaryAnne, instilled in her children a love for nature. She encouraged Thom to look at the beauty around him, to look beyond and to discover

Thom on the cross-country train trip.

what was on the other side. Thom's art has evolved into what it is today as a result of those youthful years in Placerville when venturing out led to discovering and experiencing nature's wonder in all its glory. "Everything I experience ends up in the art sooner or later," says Thom. "That is one of the reasons why I have always enjoyed traveling. Seeing new places can inspire new visual directions. Every region has its own color palette, and I think it's good to bombard your senses with different geographic areas as a means of triggering a new emotional response."

His first grand excursion to "bombard" his senses was a cross-country trek with James Gurney. The two young artists came up with the idea to cross the country by hitching rides on the rail, sketching as they went. Upon returning from the trip they decided to record their insightful adventure in the book *The Artist's Guide to Sketching*, hiring

themselves out as background artists for *Fire and Ice* to fund their time spent writing the manuscript. This 3,000-mile journey with his college pal cemented the idea in Thom that adventuring was a critical element to creative expression. A few years later those thoughts were further exemplified when the opportunity arose for yet another grand escapade. This time it was a chance for the artist to see Alaska, one of the most magnificent natural locations on the planet.

The trip to Alaska took place in the first years of his marriage. Thom joined his dealer from Phoenix, Steve Rose, who often took excursions into the wilderness, and flew over parts of the state in a float plane with Hoppy Harrower, a dentist who led pack trips on the side. Thom took them up on the invitation and spent ten days in an Alaskan winter painting in plein air in the freezing snow. It was exhilarating! He returned with a wealth of

HARROWER'S CAMP

Cover of the book, "The Artist's Guide to Sketching" written by Thom and James Gurney after their cross country trip together.

James Gurney with Thom and Nanette on a painting trip in England, 1987.

Thom and Nanette on a trip to Europe.

Photograph taken of an English cottage while plein air painting in Europe.

ideas for paintings. Out of this trip came his Alaskan series of gold towns: *Dawson, Birth of a City*, and *Moonlight on the Riverfront*. This sensory experience proved to be a strong influence on his later landscapes and sparked his desire to plan future distant artistic adventures.

"When we'd been married just a few years," recalls Nanette, "we had a desire to go to Europe to paint in England and France—to plein air paint throughout Europe." And so began the next great adventure. Without any real funds, the couple needed to think of an innovative way to raise the money for the trip. Fortunately, they were able to secure the use of a mobile home and old RV by trading one of Thom's paintings in exchange for the rental fees, and off they drove through the European

Finished painting of the same English cottage shown at left.

countryside. During this trip Thom painted more than twenty plein airs of English cottages and European landscapes. The experience enriched his overall subject matter. "When I was in England," remembers Thom, "I found my work gaining a new intimacy. England is not about vast spaces; everything seems up close and personal. I began to paint space in a new way. A sense of mystery began to emerge in the compositions, the kind of mystery that you feel as you embark on a treasure hunt. There is that joyous sense of discovery. In England, I constantly felt that kind of delight in what I was seeing. Around every corner was a new discovery. I think it has to do with the intense nature of southern England; because it is very wet and densely overgrown, you're constantly ducking around shrubs and bushes and finding a hidden glade or a secret garden. This sense of mystery pervades English literature, this sense of nature as an enchanted place filled with wondrous discoveries."

> "When I travel with Thom, I make sure to be totally prepared for the unexpected."
>
> —Rick Barnett

The abundance of captivating scenery that Thom and Nanette experienced on their eye-opening trip to Europe is one of the reasons why Thom never travels without being fully prepared for an exciting art encounter. At all times he carries with him a specially designed backpack and a unique easel, which he designed himself from a camera tripod. "When I travel with Thom, I make sure to be totally prepared for the unexpected," says Rick Barnett. "You just never know when you're traveling with him whether or not the car's going to stop and suddenly it's time for a two-hour break while he paints some glorious subject matter that he didn't expect to see." One such trip was in Austria. Though the day had been planned differently, after a trip to an antique store, Thom decided on an impromptu visit to a small village in the Alps, Heiligen Blut, a five-hour drive from Salzburg. As the car reached the crest of the mountaintop, Thom could see the village in the valley below. The little village of Heiligen Blut was absolutely breathtaking to the passengers in the car as the sun was just about to spill over into the valley. Thom climbed out of the vehicle in 20-degree weather and

"He has a wonderful sense of humor . . . some of the paintings he did in England look very serene, and in reality the act of painting them was nothing like that!"—Donna Pace

set up his easel. It was so cold that he had to snip off the fingertips of his new gloves just so that he could hold the paintbrush while still protecting most of his hand from the frigid air.

For Thom, all of these impromptu excursions are worth it for the sheer joy they bring to the overall experience. "Every day I wake up," he says, "I step outside and smell the air and look at the mist on the mountains and say to myself, 'Life is amazing!' I truly am in awe of the experience of living. When I hear people say that they are bored, I can only think that they need to adjust their mindset and begin exploring. There is so much to discover if you only have the energy to reach out to new experiences." For Thom, the best part of any day is being able to see something new and then transfer the moment onto canvas. There is something special about the plein air tradition of painting. Artists view plein air work as sacred ground, not only because of its spontaneity but because each artist begins at the same starting point, on equal terms. "To watch Thom take a two- to three-hour

period to capture his impression of something onto canvas is magical," recounts Rick Barnett. "It's incredible to see a white canvas take shape—dimension, form, light, color; all of that gets translated onto canvas." Like Thomas Kinkade, past plein air artists such as Guy Rose, Edgar Payne, and the California impressionists set up their canvases as quickly as possible upon seeing a spectacular sight and rushed to capture the light before it faded, capture the mood before it changed, all following the same inspirational formula to tell the story of what they saw before it disappeared behind a cloud. For an artist, like a writer, is a consummate storyteller.

Thom's sense of fun and adventure and his joy of life seem to engulf every canvas that he runs a paintbrush

across. Each painting has a story behind the picture that few ever hear. "Thom is a wonderful storyteller," says Donna Pace. "He has a wonderful sense of humor and is not afraid to laugh at himself or admit foibles. When you look at some of the paintings he did in England, they look very serene, and in reality the act of painting them was nothing like that! For instance, he brought back one that had a beautiful, rippling, little brook and a pretty little bridge; it turns out that the name of the stream is Slaughter, and he had to run away from the spot twice before the man who owned it finally stopped threatening to call the constable and allowed him to paint!" Such humorous stories are behind many of his plein airs. Once, when he was painting San Francisco

Finished plein air painting of the seaside in Greece.

Painting on a mountaintop in the Sierras, 1999.

In Israel painting the Via Dolorosa while two Israeli boys watch, 2006.

Photograph taken in Greece while painting plein air by the sea.

In Yosemite with Nanette on a painting trip, 1983.

Bay's Alcatraz Island, the angle that Thom needed required him to access the end of a pier that had a large "off limits" sign posted on it. Ever the stickler for the perfect vantage point, Thom persisted, trying three times to sneak out to the pier's end, each time getting caught and sent away from the area. Eventually, Thom was able to talk a kindly old watchman into allowing him to scoot in at the side. Even after being granted access to the area, he still had to paint the scene as if he were competing on a television game show. He knew that at any moment the old man's boss would arrive and kick him out again. "Thom doesn't have a malicious bone in his body," says Donna Pace. "When he tells his stories, it's always with such an enjoyment of the people that are around him." That is always part of the adventure for Thom: meeting the people along the way.

A very social man who relishes in the company of others, Thomas Kinkade enjoys having people participate with him in life. "Thom is an engaging kind of a person," says Ken Raasch, co-founder of Lightpost Publishing. "He brings people along with him. He is a person that thrives on experience, whether it's riding horses in the mountains, going to Hawaii or just waking up in the morning and spending time with the kids. He loves the experience.

He loves people. I've told him he's the most unlikely character to be an artist—somebody who has to sit for ten to twelve hours a day and paint by himself—because he's so gregarious and he enjoys people so much." One of the most deeply personal of these "people experiences" that Thom will never forget was the time he went to Europe with his brother, Pat, and his father, Bill.

Thom and Pat traveled with their father on a poignant trip to Europe, visiting the sites that Bill had toured as a young soldier in World War II. As brothers, as sons, and as men, they talked to their father about his wartime experiences, which he recounted in vivid detail. "When our dad went up that beach," recounts

Thom with father, Bill, and Pat on their WWII tour of Europe.

Pat, "for him that was his defining moment. Outside of his family, that was the most important thing that he had ever accomplished in his life, being involved with the war effort. Trying to get hold of that perspective, of him as a man, not just our dad, was relatively elusive, but that trip provided significant insight."

The best kind of adventuring for Thom is the unplanned kind. *Serendipity* is a term that he is fond of using. The unexpected moment should be grabbed and courageously lived, and laughter is vitally important. For Thom, there is always an adventure waiting to happen at any given moment. "Thom has such an ability to make little things a celebration just through an attitude of the heart," says Nanette. "It's always very exciting. Thom makes every day special where there's always something to look forward to. For instance, our daily jog: It's not just about burning calories; it's an adventure to see the new growth on the trees. It's an attitude of life he has, a way of bringing enthusiasm to the mundane."

Friends have often said that everywhere Thom goes somehow it turns into a vacation. "Even his favorite form of recreation is going out and painting," shares Nanette. "He'll take his paints when we go out on a hike or take a little adventure and do a plein air painting." Whether he is picnicking

Thom, Pat, and friends on a horseback trip to paint in the Sierras, 1999.

"*His favorite form of recreation is painting. He'll take his paints when we go out on a hike or take a little adventure and do a plein air painting.*"—Nanette Kinkade

with his wife and children or heading off to the beach, part of the enjoyment of the trip is the time spent sketching or painting what he finds. How wonderful to make your living doing what you love! Thom thinks the ability to see beauty and then interpret it on a canvas is the very best way to do a vacation."

Capturing the exact moment on canvas—the moment that glorifies and accentuates the light—is especially significant for Thom. "I've never gone more than a week without picking up a paint brush in the last thirty-five years," he says. "I've even set my easel up in a hotel room when I had a project I wanted to focus on. I remember bringing my easel camping once and, on the day it rained, working inside a pup tent. I suppose it becomes a form of obsession because it's a very

fulfilling experience. You are seeing the results right before your eyes as you work. It's not like writing. With painting, it's instantaneous." It is that moment of exhilarating joy that he shares most often with his wife, Nanette. "My wife had one of those moments as we were cross-country skiing beside Lake Tahoe," recalls Thom. "We came upon a broad snowy field and the light began breaking through from the clouds. Off in the distance, the sunlight lay upon a patch of snow and was moving towards us. I turned to her, but before I could make a comment, I noticed she was in tears. 'It is just so beautiful,' she said."

Every day is an adventure that holds a miracle, Thom says, if we just take time to notice. "I believe it is necessary to not drift through the experiences of life, but to have your radar up to catch those fleeting moments of divine inspiration—moments when it just seems as though the world is more splendid than can be described."

Thom in Tahoe painting in the snow, 1990's.

TOWER BRIDGE, LONDON

The play

of light on water, the glorious

glow of sunlight reflected,

and the radiant sense

of movement and life are part

of the unpredictable, ever-

changing world

of plein air painting.

BLOOMSBURY CAFÉ

EDINBURGH, SCOTLAND

This is a city of almost magical charm. I've never had so strong

a sense of the living Middle Ages as I did when I sat before my easel overlooking Edinburgh's famed Old Town.

CASHEL ROCK, IRELAND

Rhine Valley

LAKE LUCERNE

NEUSCHWANSTEIN

HEILIGEN BLUT

Silence and tranquility

are portrayed in this winter masterpiece set in a secluded Austrian town.

NICE, FRENCH RIVIERA

NOTRE DAME, PARIS

ISLAND AFTERNOON, GREECE

The via

Dolorosa was identified

during the Middle Ages as

the route along which

Christ carried His cross.

I set my easel at the very spot

commemorating where

Christ received His

crown of thorns.

VIA DOLOROSA

PORTOFINO

Catalina, View from Descano

PACIFIC GROVE

Wherever

I went, I saw the way

the light played through

the trees, on the vegetation,

everywhere. This is an

example of my exploration

of playing with light

on canvas.

Capitola Village

LAKE ARROWHEAD

UNION SQUARE, SAN FRANCISCO

PALM SPRINGS

One of the early galleries showing my art was in the Southwest.

I love the surprise of the desert's color and light where others might have imagined there was none.

KEY WEST

I have hidden a number of world figures in this scene,

most notable, Ernest Hemingway, who stands in front of Sloppy Joe's Bar. Between ten and twenty layers of paint,

featuring delicate glazing, create the opalescent hues of the Caribbean.

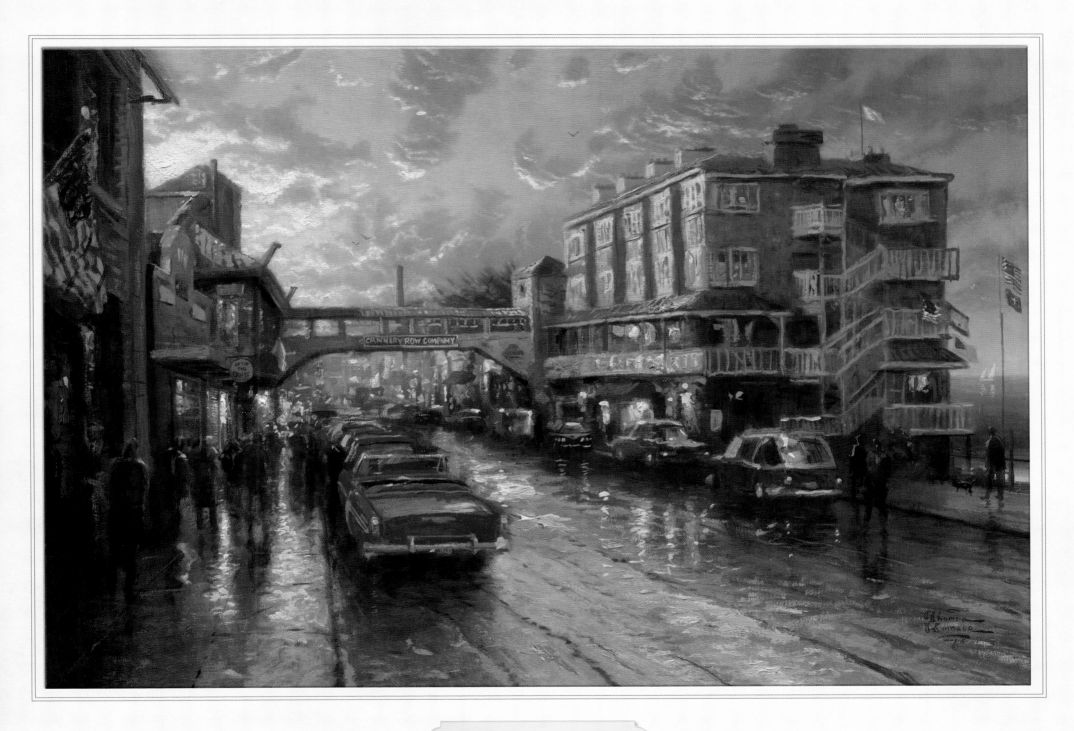

CANNERY ROW SUNSET

PLAZA LIGHTS, KANSAS CITY

During

the Great Chicago Fire

of 1871, the Water Tower was

among the few buildings in

the city that survived intact. It

inspired the citizens to build their

town bigger and better than ever.

It is now a monument to the "can

do" spunk of this "city with

big shoulders."

THE WATER TOWER, CHICAGO

RAINBOW ROW, CHARLESTON

In this picturesque section of Charleston, South Carolina,

the pinks and yellows and grays of the weathered walls meld into a pastel rainbow of rich earth tones.

In this tribute to a very special town, I included a selection of nostalgic fifties cars.

JACKSON STREET, CAPE MAY

WAVERLY ABBEY HOUSE

TREES BY THE WATER

"I am blessed that I can trace

the illumination and guidance of my life to

a single source—the love of God. Beyond that,

and most assuredly as a result of which, I have my

family. Over the course of my life, and at different

times, my family has served as anchor, pillar, haven,

and inspiration. Without them, without my childhood

family as well as the family I have been blessed

to create with Nanette, I would never have been

able to accomplish anything of significance."

Chapter Four

PUTTING DOWN ROOTS

Family and Home

HOMETOWN MORNING

> *"Step back from the fast pace of modern life and take a rest, take a walk in the park, have a picnic with your family, go fishing with some friends."* —Thomas Kinkade

MARYANNE KINKADE RAISED HER CHILDREN TO KNOW

that the sanctuary of the home is being able to close the door when everyone is inside and it's warm and safe, there is enough food on the table, and you simply love one another. The importance of cherishing family was something that Thom learned at an early age. Family is paramount to him, a message that he continually communicates in his art, his books, and his public appearances. Growing up in a single-parent home, with his mother being the sole provider and his sister, Kate, helping out with the caregiving, Thom learned a rock-solid appreciation for family. "It might be because of the lack of a normal family unit growing up," recalls his brother Pat. "I mean, we grew up in a time when single-parent households weren't very common. All of our friends had in-house dads that were available to them at any given time. I think that affected Thom in a lot of ways. He more than anything wants people to appreciate the solidarity and the comfort of having people

around that are yours no matter what. I see it in his art and I see it in his words." Ultimately it was young Nanette Willey in whom Thom realized his ideal of home and family.

The young couple met in Placerville when Nanette was twelve and Thom was thirteen. They felt a deep connection from the moment they met and soon became the best of friends. "I went on the newspaper route with him every day," recounts Nanette. "We'd go down our street to a large oak tree at the end of the road and read the funny papers and talk. He'd come by the house and we'd jump on the trampoline and talk. We spent a lot of time talking and dreaming. It's very interesting to look back and see how many of the things that we talked and dreamed about at those very, very early ages, have come to pass. We even dreamed about being married and having a family."

Nanette wanted to be a nurse. Her career choice had a lot to do with having lived in a

number of different countries with her family and being able to see how others lived. One year while in the Philippines, her family visited a mountain hospital where Nanette witnessed

Thom and Nanette, 1999.

"The most important thing that Thom and I share together is a friendship." —Nanette Kinkade

a village woman giving birth. It affected her so greatly that from that time on she decided to enter the profession. Like Nanette, Thom knew what he wanted, and that was to be an artist. By the time he met Nanette art was already a fundamental part of his character. The two spent their teen years together in Placerville and built a strong friendship before heading in different directions by the time the college years rolled around. They decided it would be in their best interest to break off the relationship and focus on the path their lives might take individually. Nanette went to Chico State University to study nursing while Thom headed off to Berkeley and then Pasadena where he enrolled in the Art Center College of Design. "Being the same grade in school, Nanette and I shared more mutual circles," remembers Pat. "Thom would always be calling from Los Angeles and no matter what we would talk about eventually, at the end of the conversation, he would say, 'Hey Pat, what's the Nanette situation?' So I was basically the mole into Nanette's life throughout the years that they were separated, keeping Thom abreast of anything that was going on with her so he could act immediately should the catastrophe arise that she became seriously involved with somebody."

Thom wasn't going to let anything like that happen. One summer day he came up to Placerville for a visit and decided to stop by the Willeys' house to see if Nanette was at home. "Lo and behold she's home with her leg in a cast! Thom asks her out. They go up to Tahoe and that was it. They went dancing," chuckles Thom's mother, MaryAnne as she imagines her daughter-in-law trying to dance with a cast on. "It was quite a deal. By that time I was living in Missouri and Thom contacted me and told me they were engaged. I was so happy." The young couple was married in 1982 in a little miner's church in Coloma, California. Six years later, they had their first child.

"From the beginning," says MaryAnne, "she was perfect for him. She supported him when he was struggling by working as a nurse, and he was determined to make a go of it because he loved her so much." Nanette was Thom's partner in everything. Coming home from shifts at the hospital, she helped stretch canvases for him. Even today, she often helps Thom during their plein air excursions, sorting paint and doing whatever else he might need. "The most important thing that Thom and I share together is a friendship," says Nanette. "We've made that a priority even with the busy demands that come with having a family. Before

we had children, we set a pattern of making it a priority to spend time with each other. We still have a date once a week. It's always anticipated. We plan it, dress up for it, and make it really special. Our friendship is one that over the years continues to grow in depth. The experiences that we have together keep enriching that friendship." Even today the two feel especially privileged to be able to have the arrangement that they have, with Thom's studio right next to their home, allowing them to have lunch together and take a jog every day. In the evening if Thom needs to paint late, Nanette can go over and read to him or help tidy up the studio.

Though some perceive Thom as a great artist who achieved fame overnight, the real truth is that nothing was easily attained, and it may have never been attained at all without Nanette, the person who helped keep Thom centered. Thom is a person with an immense capacity for moving in several directions at once. With Nanette in his life, he was able to remain focused. Even during the periods before success came, when Thom absolutely knew he was meant to be an artist and everyone else was saying, "Hey, maybe your husband should get a normal job. He might be able to drive a truck and get $20 an hour," Nanette would have none of it. She shared her husband's vision from the beginning and has always been his staunchest supporter. Now with four daughters, the Kinkades are living out that vision with the family they dreamed about having when they were children.

In England, painting a family affair, 1991.

Thom and Nanette with 2 daughters, Chandler and Merritt, 1991.

At the harbor with 3 daughters, baby Winsor on back

At the beach, walking toddler Merritt.

"This Is Your Life"
THOMAS KINKADE

Happy 40th Birthday!

*Inn at Spanish Bay Resort
Pebble Beach, California
January 17, 1998*

Thom's 40th Birthday Invitation.

Chandler and Merritt painting in Dad's studio.

Thom, Nanette, and daughters at Ivy Gate Studio.

"I never dreamed that we'd have four daughters," says Nanette. "We are so delighted, but I have to admit I still pinch myself and wonder how I got here with four children. Four is a large family, but it's a lot of fun. There's never a dull moment." Thom's love of life spills out into his family life and his sense of humor is always handy. Ken Raasch, who also has four children, recalls the childlike fun Thom has when he's around kids: "Our two families tend to spend Christmas Eve together as a tradition. Every Christmas Eve we'll have presents for the kids, and Thom, and Nanette will slip away, and Thom will come back dressed as Santa. The older kids know it's Thom, while the younger kids are so excited that Santa has arrived. We, of course, are trying to maintain a straight face while Thom is just cutting up and being a very mischievous Santa. But that's the kind of enjoyment of life that Thom has."

The joy of family and its importance as the central theme in his life are readily seen in his artwork. "When he paints these houses, he sees a family inside them," says MaryAnne Kinkade. "You can tell. The smoke's rising out of the chimney, the lights are glowing in the cottage windows, and for Thom this is a family, a group that stays together. I think that's part of the simpler times that most of us yearn for." The feeling of warmth and peace that people feel when

they view Thom's art is an outgrowth of the rich experience of family life that he shares with his wife and children. It's an emotion that he has learned to capture. And it is an experience that he has learned to protect.

The demands on the time of an artist of such notoriety are great. Television, radio,

newspapers, magazines, art galleries, and companies that license Thomas Kinkade images all want a piece of his time. Through the years Thom has learned to balance these demands, always keeping family front and center. He has learned to recognize that there is a hard line that needs to be drawn between the demands of his business and an unacceptable drain of his

focus on his family. "Probably the only time I've ever seen Thom get a little twitchy or nervous," says Rick Barnett, "is when he's reaching that line where he feels that the demands on his time are taking a toll on the kind of focus he wants to have on his family. But he's good at being able to say, 'I can do this and this, but I can't do these other things because those things would come at the expense of my family.'"

Thom's belief that family time is crucial, that people should often step back from the fast pace of modern life and enjoy the simpler things, is a message that resonates with millions of people. As technology becomes better and we look for slimmer computers, higher-definition TVs, faster cars, and software programs that can run every part of our lives, Thomas Kinkade says, "Step back from all of that and take a rest, take a walk in the park, have a picnic with your family, go fishing with some friends." That is the core message of his artwork. It is in complete contrast to the hustle-and-bustle world that many of us get caught up in. People are drawn to his images for the simple reason that they remind us of a special time. If they can't experience simplicity in their own lives, at least they can experience it via a Thomas Kinkade image. Thom and Nanette try to instill in their own children the importance of serenity and simplicity. They don't own a television and often spend their time outdoors, picnicking, hiking, horseback riding, traveling to beaches, and just enjoying the uncomplicated things in life.

HOMETOWN MEMORIES

VICTORIAN GARDEN II

HIDDEN COTTAGE

HOME IS WHERE THE HEART IS

I enjoy the look of charming two-story homes such as this.

As I worked on this painting, I imagined my own family living in this beautiful setting.

Sunday Outing

Family traditions. A favorite of ours is the Sunday drive.

After church we'll take off in the family car, often driving in California's Apple Hill country.

HOME IS WHERE THE HEART IS II

My

English cottage paintings

have always been my attempt

to reach into the deepest part

of my emotions—those hidden

joyous fantasies we all have of

places more special than

our everyday world.

THE BLUE COTTAGE

CHANDLER'S COTTAGE

THE BLESSINGS OF SUMMER

LOCHAVEN COTTAGE

At twilight, a hush falls over the countryside,

the wind stills, the surface of a small lake calms to mirror smoothness, reflecting the brilliant hues of sunset.

BEYOND SPRING GATE

BEYOND AUTUMN GATE

VICTORIAN AUTUMN

The fourth seasonal addition to my series of idyllic family retreats visits

an imposing Victorian mansion in the fall. Light pours through the windows, providing a glimpse of the family life within.

GINGERBREAD COTTAGE

MOONLIGHT COTTAGE

STILLWATER COTTAGE

Carefully observed details—the weathered brass bell over the door, the ancient stone bench with an open Bible, and the graceful gliding swans—give this cottage, this place of refuge, its character.

A Quiet Evening

A New Day Dawning

Christmas Cottage

A Holiday Gathering

Of all the holiday rituals, the one I prize the most is the coming together
of loved ones in shared celebration. The Christmas season is when we pause to savor traditions of comfort and joy.

VICTORIAN CHRISTMAS

VICTORIAN CHRISTMAS II

VILLAGE CHRISTMAS

HOME FOR THE HOLIDAYS

Christmas Moonlight

In the snowy grip of winter this Christmas scene depicts the cottage
featured in *Victorian Garden II*. The cheerful snowman with his red scarf embodies the spirit of the season.

A Peaceful Retreat

MOUNTAIN RETREAT

THE END OF A PERFECT DAY

The paintings in my "day's end" collection express my growing
appreciation for the real beauty of nature untamed. They celebrate the majesty of God's creation.

THE END OF A PERFECT DAY II

THE END OF A PERFECT DAY III

MOUNTAIN PARADISE

"I see my artwork as an extension

of God's light—my paintbrush is His,

and this to me is an honor, a joy, to light

a fresh candle every day for the world with the

artwork I create. In a way, I see that I am

offering my mind, my skill, my creativity as

instruments of the divine process of remaking

the world into a better place."

Chapter Five

SHARING THE LIGHT

Charity and Faith

BRIDGE OF FAITH

> *"I think passion is the greatest gift one human can give to another. I always tell my children that if they find someone who loves God, loves them, and loves life, you have someone worth keeping."—Thomas Kinkade*

IN A QUIET, SIMPLE GESTURE OF FAITH, THOMAS

Kinkade yielded his artwork to God when he was a newly married man. He asked God to be his art agent and from that moment forward he had a mission. "Thom was always an excellent technician," says Rick Barnett. "And, giving credit to artists worldwide, there are many artists that are excellent technicians, but it wasn't until Thom let God be his art agent that his craft went beyond that of technical excellence and became a messenger of hope, love and peace." It is these messages embodied in subjects of faith, family, and simpler times that find their way into Thom's paintings. He sees his art as a vehicle to touch people's lives with the same hope and joy that he has found in his faith. His faith has been a tremendous source of inspiration and a catalyst for his creative genius. "Thom is clear on who the artist really is," continues Rick, "and it's not him. His hand is used, but he truly believes that God is the source of his inspiration. When

Thom made that big step from just being the artist who was an excellent technician to the artist that belongs to God, his work took on a completely different meaning." For Thom, the mission was clear: he was to use the creative means given to him in the service of others. It is a journey that has evolved through the years from simply blessing individuals and families with a painting that brings a bit more beauty into their world into having a larger national and global outlook, using his notoriety in whatever way possible to assist World Vision, Make-A-Wish Foundation®, and the many other charities that he has been involved with.

Thom's first involvement with charity began in his small hometown of Placerville. He painted *Placerville, Main Street, 1916* in 1984 to benefit the Placerville library for the El Dorado County Friends of the Library. The original, approximately 3 feet by 4 feet, hangs in the library to this day. "Thom has always

had an interest in giving back to those around him," says Donna Pace. "The first time that I officially met him was at a benefit for a group that was trying to get a cultural art center built in Placerville. He's done many benefits that I've been involved in. He continues to give

Thom at Children's Better Health Fair with a child who won a drawing contest, 2002.

back a great deal." His charitable interests have helped not only Placerville, but also El Dorado County and the surrounding area, from the Boys & Girls Clubs to the local hospitals.

After he partnered with Ken Raasch and started up the publishing company, their vision to use art to change people's lives continued. Lightpost Publishing's first major gift was to Rotary International. After meeting with Rotary International at their headquarters in Illinois, Thom was honored to be given the right to have his painting, *The Rotary Club Meeting*, used as the first official charity piece sold to Rotary Club members, with all proceeds given to their various charities. That print is still being sold today and has raised hundreds of thousands of dollars for charity. It was thrilling to see what good one small painting could do, so Thom continued in this direction.

Upon joining hands with World Vision, Thom took his family on a trip to Guatemala to see first-hand the needs of Guatemalan children who lived in the city and in the remote mountainous areas. The trip changed his life and added even more to his sense of

urgency to use his art in some way to help. "Thom has a deep sense of mission in his work," says his wife, Nanette, "and it revolves around his desire to reach people with God's love." Together with the Thomas Kinkade dealers who own Thomas Kinkade Galleries

"The Rotary Club Meeting"– Thom was the first official artist for the Rotary Club in 1990. This charity piece has raised hundreds of thousands of dollars for the Rotary Club's charities and is sold exclusively to Rotary Club members.

worldwide, Thom sold the image *Bridge of Faith* as an Open Edition product to raise money for World Vision. It was a major success and raised enough money to build a library and medical center in Guatemala, and 60,000 child sponsors were added to World Vision's rosters. "Thom has always found a great joy in blessing others with his art," continues Nanette. "I think its part of the fuel that keeps him going in the quest to paint the next piece."

Through his 20 Years of Light Tour, Thom has raised more than $1.2 million for the Make-A-Wish Foundation® and granted twelve wishes for children with life-threatening medical conditions. Two paintings were created to help the Salvation Army with its relief efforts for the victims of Ground Zero: *The Season of Giving* and *The Light of Freedom*, which was used as a poster in 2002. In *The Season of Giving*, Thom added a Salvation Army bell ringer in the picture as a quaint reminder of how this charitable organization has become an iconic part of our national Christmas celebration. These two images combined raised more than $2 million for the Salvation Army. Habitat for Humanity is another charity that has been close to Thom's heart. A percentage

At Children's Hospital, 2005.

With Pat Robertson, 1996.

Autographing children's caps at an event, 1998.

In a Guatemalan mountain village on a trip with World Vision, 1999.

At a 911 event. (Photo courtesy of Encourage America)

At Crystal Cathedral, sharing God's message, 1997.

With Robert Goodwin and George Bush, Sr., 2005— Thom was nominated Ambassador of Light for the Points of Light Foundation, the 2nd Ambassador after Bush, Sr. (Photo courtesy of the Points of Light Foundation)

With Billy Graham, presenting him with a painting, 1997.

of all proceeds from the limited edition lithograph, *Hometown Pride*, were given to the charity to support its home-building efforts.

As Thom's message of peace, hope, and faith continues to gain momentum through the success of his artwork, his reputation as an ambassador of goodwill becomes more commonly known. In 2005, Thom was nominated the Ambassador of Light for the Points of Light Foundation, an organization that encourages volunteerism in America. The organization's founder and first Ambassador was President George Bush, Sr., so Thom felt especially privileged to be the second one to hold the distinguished title. In 2006, he created a special painting for the Points of Light Foundation that benefited the victims of Hurricane Katrina. With the Points of Light Foundation, he became involved with the National Conference for Volunteer Service, spending a day teaching art to kids from the inner city in Washington D.C. He loves children and believes that it should be our priority to keep the creative arts alive in schools. "I think drawing is the first language, not speech," says Thom. "I believe a fascination with scribbling and drawing becomes a defining point in a child's life because a blank piece of paper and a crayon are completely empowering to an individual. You are in charge of the creative act. I like to watch over the shoulders of children as they draw and paint. There is complete freedom there that is very compelling."

This image was created for the Points of Light Foundation to help raise money for Hurricane Katrina victims.

Over the years he has brought his paints to hospitals, schools, health fairs, and other events, sharing his passion for art with the next generation of young artists, not only showing them the joy of being creative but, he hopes, sharing the light of God's love in a simple, unpretentious manner. Sharing has always been part of Thom's mission; he loves talking to and explaining art to people, even to children. It has always been important to him to give to the community, not just with financial support but also with his expertise and passion, so the understanding of art is expanded. Thom is committed to bringing an appreciation of beauty to those around him.

Thom sees his art as a form of ministry and excitedly shares his faith at the many places he is invited to speak. Whether it is

157

"Thom wants the joy in his heart to be transmitted to those who view his work."—Nanette Kinkade

to a larger audience at Crystal Cathedral or at a smaller gallery event, Thom doesn't hesitate to share what he feels is the source of his inspiration. "My brother is a man of mature faith," says Pat Kinkade. "There may be people who have more technical knowledge or historical data, but I've never seen anybody have as much certainty about what he believes in as Thom. Trying to convey that peace that he enjoys through his faith is another one of his messages."

Some have said that Thom's paintings are messengers of hope that go into people's homes, and there have been many instances where a collector has shared a moment of profound healing or joy during a difficult time of life by simply looking at a Thomas Kinkade painting. His use of light on the canvas is one way in which he communicates the spiritual values in his life and offers a joyful interlude to the viewing audience at the same time. "Thom wants the joy that he has in his heart to be transmitted to those who view his work," says Nanette. "The major impact that we've seen through Thom's work is the amount of hope that people find in it. I think that is an outgrowth of the hope that he feels in his own heart." The first seedlings of such hope were planted in him as a young child when he began

to feel a connection to God through the beauty he saw around him in the fields and woods of Placerville, a city that became the setting for many of Thom's works. But it was his mother, MaryAnne, who had the greatest influence on the direction Thom's faith would take.

As a woman of faith herself, she was a pillar of strength to her small family. MaryAnne's advice for mothering is to love your children because they hunger for it, pray because you need help, and keep the Lord first, then your family. While overcoming great adversity in her own life, she developed a faith that she passed on to her children, faithfully taking them to church and reading the bible to them. "It's such a joy to have a child who you can speak about the Lord to and share experiences," says MaryAnne, commenting on Thom's faith. "And I'm delighted that my children are developing that because it's for their own blessing and for their own good."

In every area of his life, Thom would say, his faith has played a major role. "Probably his greatest gift," says Nanette, "is the gift of faith that he has. When he has a vision for something he doesn't let loose of that even when things don't look like they're going to go well. He has been a continual encouragement in our family." His faith and passion for life

not only are reflected in his paintings, but are reflected in his own family. "I think passion is the greatest gift one human can give to another," says Thom. "I live life with a high degree of passion. I always tell my children that if they find someone who loves God, loves them, and loves life, you have someone worth keeping. A love for God gives your life purpose, a love for life gives your life joy, and a love for a person gives your life fullness. There is no greater lesson for my children than to cherish the most precious of all gifts: the gift of life." His optimistic view of the world is not based on circumstances. Thom would say it is an attitude that is carefully nurtured and can be found by anyone in any situation. A thankful heart is the wellspring of joy, and that, too, springs from his faith.

When Thom is gone and the legacy of his paintings remains, some say he will not be thought of as the "painter of great trees" or the "painter of great buildings"; he will be viewed as the painter of his time, who interpreted that which he saw in the world in a very positive light. If his goal was to become a part of as many people's lives as possible, then he is an unparalleled success because his art is enjoyed by so many people throughout the world. Thom's desire is that through his paintings people will be encouraged to reprioritize their lives, perhaps causing them to change directions, slow down, choose family over outside influences, and look for beauty in the smallest of things.

A love

for God gives your life

purpose, a love for life gives

your life joy, and a love

for a person gives your life

fullness. I pray my *Sunrise*

painting will be symbolic

of a new dawning of

God's grace and love

in the years ahead.

SUNRISE

STAIRWAY TO PARADISE

THE GARDEN OF PRAYER

BRIDGE OF HOPE

MAKE A WISH COTTAGE

For all the children who dare to dream,

I created Make A Wish Cottage, a sanctuary where dreams can come true.

FRIENDSHIP COTTAGE

LIVING WATERS, GOLFER'S PARADISE, HOLE ONE

"If there were a golf course in Heaven ..."

Like many people of faith, I have often contemplated the glories of Heaven. Imagine the possibilities: not a care to interrupt a fragrant walk through the morning light as one pursues the perfect round.

A Garden

with a rambling stone

walkway climbing up through

flower hedges represents my

tribute to the hope many of

us share of the better times

that lie ahead.

THE GARDEN OF PROMISE

POOLS OF SERENITY

Before

we ever began to build

temples in His honor, God

graced us with natural

sanctuaries radiant with

the light of divine

love and peace.

THE MOUNTAIN CHAPEL

SUNRISE CHAPEL

THE FOREST CHAPEL

BLOSSOM HILL CHURCH

I have a fondness for all country churches.

I'm particularly attached to Blossom Hill Church; within its weathered walls my wife and I were wed!

The hope

that pervades this painting

is a profound reminder that

through fervent prayer, each

of us might find peace for

our soul first, and perhaps

for our world as well.

A PRAYER FOR PEACE

THE GOOD SHEPHERD'S COTTAGE

BEACON OF HOPE

The Glory

of God's love surrounds us, the
grace of God's love comforts us,
and the strength of God's love
lifts us up, all reminding us
He is the light of the world.
As an art student in 1980,
I came to have a personal
relationship with Christ.
Struck with a powerful vision,
this image was laid upon my
heart, and I created
this painting.

THE PRINCE OF PEACE

CONQUERING THE STORMS

PERSEVERANCE

A Light in the Storm

THE LIGHT OF PEACE

God's glorious light streams through the clouds in brilliant beams.

That moment—when peace returns to the land, the sea, and the sky—is a wonderful affirmation that all storms will end.

THE SEASON OF GIVING

Created as a charity piece for the Salvation Army
to help in its relief efforts for the victims of Ground Zero, this painting is actually a vignette
of *Village Christmas* and was enhanced by adding a Salvation Army bell ringer.

SUNDAY EVENING SLEIGH RIDE

THE LIGHTS OF LIBERTY

The hero

of this painting is not an

individual at all; he is the essence

of the American soldier.

The weight of all he has seen and

done bear down on his broad

shoulders. This soldier's personal

war is over; he is heading home.

We can only wish him a joyful

homecoming, and say a word

of thanks to the heroes

of every generation!

HEADING HOME

FLAGS OVER THE CAPITOL

My pride in America and what we stand for, my love for my fellow man, and my faith in God were the inspirations for this painting. Now is the time when each of us must summon our courage and strength so that the "Light of Freedom" will forever illuminate this glorious country. God bless America.

THE LIGHT OF FREEDOM